DISCOVER
DINOSAURS

Contributing Writer
Donald F. Glut

Consultant
Peter Dodson

Publications International, Ltd.

Manufactured in China.

8 7 6 5 4 3 2 1

ISBN: 0-7853-6109-X

Photo credits:
Front cover: **Luis V. Rey**
Back cover: **Luis V. Rey** (top); **Joe Tucciarone** (bottom).

American Museum of Natural History: 18 (center); **Ann Ronan Picture Library:** 5 (top & bottom), 6 (top), 35 (top); **Donald Baird:** 8 (bottom); **Ken Carpenter:** 20 (top), 21 (center), 24 (center), 33 (bottom), 34 (right center), 36 (top), 39 (top); **Dinosaur National Monument/ National Park Service:** 27 (top); **Field Museum of Natural History:** 6 (top center), 18 (bottom), 30 (bottom), 31 (center); **Brian Franczak:** Title page, contents, 4, 7 (top), 8 (top), 9 (top), 10 (top right & left center), 12 (bottom), 13 (center), 14 (bottom), 15 (top & center), 16, 18 (center), 19 (bottom), 20 (bottom), 21 (top & bottom), 22 (center), 23, 24 (top & bottom), 25 (top & center), 26, 28 (top right, center & bottom right), 30 (top), 31 (center & bottom), 32, 33 (center), 34 (top), 35 (bottom), 36 (bottom), 37 (center & bottom), 38, 39 (bottom), 42 (top & bottom), endsheets; **Patrick R. Gulley/Chicago Academy of Sciences:** 11, 28 (top left); **Douglas Henderson:** 6 (bottom center), 33 (top); **Blair Howard:** 9 (top right center); **Eleanor M. Kish/Canadian Museum of Nature:** 29, 39 (right center), 43; **Candi Marshall:** 40 (bottom); **New Mexico Museum of Natural History:** 10 (top left & bottom), 12 (top & left center), 13 (bottom); **Gregory S. Paul:** 6 (bottom), 8 (bottom left center), 12 (top right center & lower center), 13 (top left), 15 (bottom), 17, 19 (top, left center & right center), 22 (top), 25 (bottom), 28 (bottom left), 40 (right center), 41 (bottom), 42 (center); **Lorie Robare:** 5 (bottom left); **Paul Sereno:** 9 (bottom); **Bruce Shillinglaw:** 36 (center); **Mineo Shiraishi:** 9 (bottom right center), 34 (left center); **Joe Tucciarone:** 7 (bottom), 8 (center), 14 (top), 27 (bottom), 41 (top); **Tyrell Museum of Paleontology:** 37 (top); **John Sibbick:** 35 (center); **Daniel Varner:** 31 (top); **Bob Walters:** 20 (center); 36 (right center), 39 (left center), 40 (top).

Donald F. Glut is a writer, lecturer, and consultant on dinosaurs. His books include *The Dinosaur Dictionary; The Dinosaur Scrapbook;* and *Dinosaurs, Mammoths and Cavemen: The Art of Charles R. Knight.* He was also the writer, co-producer, and co-performer of *Dinosaur Tracks,* a cassette album about dinosaurs.

Peter Dodson, Ph.D., is a widely recognized expert on dinosaurs. He is the co-editor of *The Dinosauria* and author of *The Horned Dinosaurs,* as well as consultant for the *Encyclopedia of Dinosaurs.* He is professor of anatomy at the School of Veterinary Medicine and professor of paleontology, both at the University of Pennsylvania. He received his undergraduate degree from the University of Ottawa, his master's from the University of Alberta, and his doctorate from Yale University.

CONTENTS

DINOSAUR BEGINNINGS

DINOSAUR HISTORY

Dinosaurs have amazed people for thousands of years. A Chinese book written between 265 and 317 A.D. mentions "dragon bones." These bones may have been dinosaur bones. Many dinosaur bones have been found in the same area that the "dragon bones" were found.

In England, Robert Plot found a thigh bone of what was probably *Megalosaurus* in 1677, but at first he thought it was a giant human thigh bone. Later, in 1824, William Buckland wrote about a tooth-filled lower jaw of *Megalosaurus*. It was the first scientific dinosaur write-up.

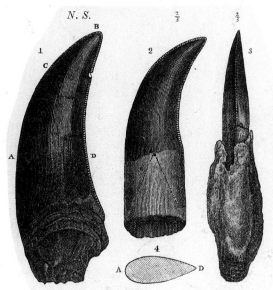

Teeth of Megalosaurus from Stonesfield, Oxon.

DINOSAUR BEGINNINGS

Cope and Marsh were not friends. Marsh showed that Cope had made mistakes in describing a marine reptile. Cope never forgot the insult.

Waterhouse Hawkins building dinosaur statues.

Above: *Apatosaurus* and *Brontosaurus* are the same dinosaur, but *Apatosaurus* was the first name. Left: *Iguanodon* was an early dinosaur discovery. Below: *Diplodocus* is a very popular dinosaur at museum exhibits.

Mary Ann Woodhouse Mantell found some large reptile teeth in 1822. At first scientists were puzzled. In 1825, Mantell's husband, Dr. Gideon Mantell, saw some teeth of an iguana lizard and realized how similar they were to large reptile teeth. He named the animal *Iguanodon* (which means "iguana's tooth"). Dr. Mantell named his second dinosaur, *Hylaeosaurus*, in 1833.

Sir Richard Owen, in 1842, studied Buckland's and Mantell's fossils and created the name *Dinosauria*, which means "terrible lizard." In 1854, Owen and Waterhouse Hawkins, an artist, built life-size models of *Megalosaurus, Iguanodon,* and *Hylaeosaurus* to put in Crystal Palace Park in England.

While many scientists in England were studying dinosaurs, America was about to start its own dinosaur rush. Two important dinosaur hunters were Othniel C. Marsh and Edward Drinker Cope. They began searching and competing to find the biggest and best skeletons. Often, their rush to describe dinosaurs led to the same dinosaur being named twice. *Apatosaurus* and *Brontosaurus* are the same animal, but with two different names!

Henry Fairfield Osborn supervised finding and preparing dinosaur skeletons for display at the American Museum. Then millionaire Andrew Carnegie gave a lot of money to a natural history museum in Pittsburgh, later named the Carnegie Museum, to get dinosaurs to put on display. Workers found two skeletons of a dinosaur, which was named *Diplodocus carnegii,* in Wyoming. The skeleton was a hit and was nicknamed "Dippy."

Since these early discoveries, many more dinosaurs have been found. These early explorers, along with many others, laid the groundwork for later dinosaur hunters. In addition to England and the United States, Canada, Germany, Poland, Argentina, France, Japan, Mongolia, the People's Republic of China, and Russia have since sent workers to find more dinosaurs.

Paleontologists (scientists who study fossils) have found and described many skeletons, but many are still buried in the rocks. There are still countless left to be found in 20 and even 100 years. So consider the exciting and interesting world of dinosaurs as a career!

DINOSAUR CLASSIFICATION

Dinosaurs lived in the Mesozoic Era, which was divided into three periods. The Triassic Period was when dinosaurs first evolved. More and larger dinosaurs appeared in the Jurassic Period. The Cretaceous Period was when dinosaurs reached their peak.

Dinosaurs belonged to a group of reptiles called archosaurs. Crocodilians, pterosaurs, and thecodonts were also part of this group. Archosaurs appeared before the Mesozoic began, in the Permian Period. As a group, they became important at the beginning of the Mesozoic.

An important change happened to some archosaurs in the Triassic Period. Their hips and legs changed. They no longer stood like sprawling lizards, but stood with their legs held under their bodies. Also, dinosaur ancestors developed strong ankles.

There are two groups of dinosaurs—the ornithischians (the bird-hipped dinosaurs) and the saurischians (the lizard-hipped dinosaurs). Very early, primitive dinosaurs, such as *Staurikosaurus* and *Herrerasaurus*, are hard to fit in either group.

The saurischian dinosaurs were the prosauropods, the sauropods, the theropods, and the segnosaurs. Surprisingly, birds are more closely related to lizard-hipped dinosaurs than to bird-hipped dinosaurs.

Top: *Seismosaurus* has recently been scientifically described. Bottom: The top pelvis belongs to an ornithischian, or "bird-hipped" dinosaur. The bottom pelvis belongs to the saurischian, or "lizard-hipped" group.

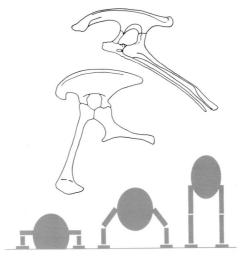

Maybe you can discover a dinosaur as large as *Seismosaurus,* which may be over 140 feet long!

Above: Archosaurs changed from sprawling animals to animals with their legs held directly underneath them. Below: *Deinonychus* was a meat-eating, saurischian dinosaur.

DINOSAUR BEGINNINGS

Riojasaurus was a Late Triassic prosauropod.

The Jurassic sauropods, including *Brachiosaurus*, were enormous. Some may have been longer than 100 feet!

Above: *Segnosaurus* is a mysterious dinosaur. Although it is a theropod, it also has some features similar to those of prosauropods. **Left:** An *Allosaurus* jaw shows the large meat-eating teeth. Many theropods had large teeth.

The prosauropods appeared in the Late Triassic and lived until the Early Jurassic. This group of dinosaurs was related to the sauropods, which appeared later. The prosauropods were large, some more than 20 feet long. The most famous of this group is *Plateosaurus*. All prosauropods ate plants.

The sauropods were giant, four-legged plant-eaters with long necks and tails. They lived in the Jurassic and the Cretaceous. The vertebrae (bones of the spine) of these huge animals had deep hollows to make them lighter. These are some of the most famous dinosaurs, including *Apatosaurus*, *Brachiosaurus*, *Diplodocus*, and *Camarasaurus*.

The theropods were a large group of meat-eaters. All the predatory (meat-eaters that hunt for food) dinosaurs belonged to this group. Theropods had advanced feet and ankles, and their feet had claws. All walked on two legs. Birds seem to be closely related to these dinosaurs. The size ranged from small, such as *Coelophysis*, to quite large, such as *Tyrannosaurus*, *Giganotosaurus*, and *Carcharodontosaurus*.

The segnosaurs are an unusual group of recently discovered dinosaurs that have been a bit of a mystery. They were found in China and Mongolia. At first, scientists thought they were meat-eaters, then they thought they were plant-eaters, but now scientists have resolved that they were right in the first place. Although this group has features in common with the plant-eating prosauropods, paleontologists have determined that segnosaurs are a strange sort of theropod.

All ornithischian dinosaurs were plant-eaters. Later ornithischians split into five different groups. Three groups walked on all fours, two groups walked on two legs.

The stegosaurs were the dinosaurs with the large plates on their backs that lived in the

DINOSAUR BEGINNINGS

Jurassic. A few also lived in the Cretaceous. *Stegosaurus* is the best-known stegosaur. China has the most kinds of stegosaurs.

The ankylosaurs appeared in the Jurassic and replaced stegosaurs in the Cretaceous. Ankylosaurs, or armored dinosaurs, had flexible body armor rather than a double row of tall plates. Where stegosaurs had spikes on their tails, some ankylosaurs had a bony club. *Ankylosaurus* is the best-known ankylosaur.

The ceratopsians (ser-a-TOP-see-inz) were the horned dinosaurs and their relatives. These animals had a special bone, called the *rostral*, which formed a parrotlike beak at the front of their mouths. The best-known ceratopsian is *Triceratops*. Many advanced ceratopsians had large, spectacular frills. A frill was a bony shelf from the back of the skull that covered the neck.

All ornithopods were two-legged plant-eaters that lived during almost the entire age of dinosaurs. The Late Cretaceous duckbills were the most advanced, with hundreds of teeth in their mouths for chewing. Some duckbills had a crest, which was a hollow or solid structure on top of their heads. Animals with hollow crests may have used them to "trumpet" to other members of their group. Some famous ornithopods were *Camptosaurus, Iguanodon, Maiasaura,* and *Corythosaurus.*

The pachycephalosaurs (PAK-ee-CEF-a-lo-SAHRS) (or bone-headed dinosaurs) were an unusual bunch of two-legged dinosaurs. They had thick skulls that they probably used in head-butting contests. They may have done this to compete for mates.

Though they ruled the world, dinosaurs died out at the end of the Cretaceous Period. They were amazing creatures—and we continue to study them millions of years after they lived.

Huayangosaurus was a Middle Jurassic stegosaur.

Stegosaur plates may have fooled predators. They may have disguised which end was which— tail or head!

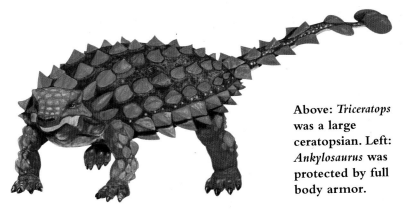

Above: *Triceratops* was a large ceratopsian. Left: *Ankylosaurus* was protected by full body armor.

This skull shows how thick the head of a pachycephalosaur was. This head belonged to *Prenocephale.*

THE TRIASSIC WORLD

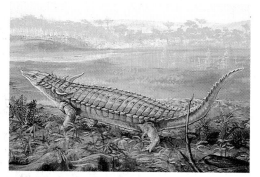

was one of change. Some animals and plants became extinct, while others evolved and thrived. These changes allowed dinosaurs to appear.

When the Triassic began, all land was connected into one continent called Pangaea. During the Triassic, Pangaea slowly moved north and turned clockwise. The eastern side of Pangaea surrounded the Tethys Sea, which was connected to a single global ocean. Because of these changes, the weather during the Triassic started out cool and dry and became warmer by the end.

Triassic plants were affected by weather, and some became extinct and others evolved. Triassic plants included ferns, conifers, and cycads, but no flowering plants were yet found.

Archosaurs had first appeared in the period before the Triassic, the Permian. The archosaurs include dinosaurs, crocodiles, pterosaurs, and thecodonts. Thecodonts were cousins of dinosaurs.

Therapsids (mammallike reptiles), which had once ruled this planet, were small and uncommon by the end of the Triassic. At the beginning, therapsids were large and abundant. *Lystrosaurus* was once a ruling therapsid, but by the middle of the Early Triassic it was no longer important. *Erythrosuchus,* a large meat-eater, and *Euparkeria,* a small, fast meat-eater, were archosaurs that became important. *Euparkeria* was important because it had features of later archosaurs.

By the Middle Triassic, archosaurs were becoming more important, and more meat-eaters were emerging. Dinosaur ancestors were beginning to be important.

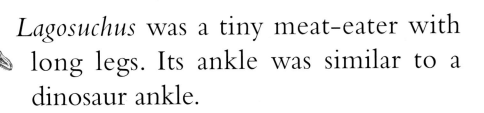

Lagosuchus was a tiny meat-eater with long legs. Its ankle was similar to a dinosaur ankle.

The first dinosaurs were found in earliest Late Triassic rocks in Brazil and Argentina. There have been three-toed, dinosaurlike footprints from as early as the end of the Early Triassic. The earliest dinosaurs we know are *Staurikosaurus, Eoraptor,* and *Herrerasaurus.* Soon after, plant-eating prosauropods, such as *Plateosaurus* and its smaller relative *Mussaurus,* were making their presence known. Theropods, including *Coelophysis,* appeared in the middle of the Late Triassic. Mammals, the descendants of therapsids, were also present in the Late Triassic.

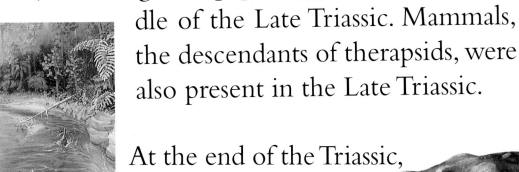

At the end of the Triassic, a large extinction took place. All archosaurs except dinosaurs, crocodilians, and pterosaurs became extinct. The scene was set for dinosaurs to become the most successful land animals.

COELOPHYSIS

(SEE-lo-PHY-sis)

Although many later theropods were giants, *Coelophysis* was about eight or nine feet long, weighing about 100 pounds.

Coelophysis was a member of the group called theropods. Theropods were meat-eaters of all sizes that walked on long hind legs and had short front legs, big heads, and sharp teeth.

relative size

A later relative of *Coelophysis* was *Syntarsus* (sin-TAR-sus), who was more advanced. It had fewer teeth, a bigger head, and weaker hands.

The head of *Coelophysis* had big eyes and a pointed snout. Dozens of knife-edged teeth lined its jaws. Its tail was long and slender and, like other dinosaurs, held off the ground. The front legs were small and (as in other theropods) not used for walking. The hind legs were long and strong. Its bones were hollow (the name *Coelophysis* means "hollow limb shaft"). Like birds' legs, those of *Coelophysis* were lightly built but strong. The feet had three long toes and one very short toe.

The hindlimbs of *Coelophysis* were made for fast movement. *Coelophysis* had to be quick on its feet to escape some of the larger meat-eating animals of its day. These bigger hunters were not dinosaurs, but huge four-footed reptiles such as the crocodilelike phytosaurs and rauisuchids.

When hunting for food, *Coelophysis* probably went after insects, lizardlike reptiles, and even other dinosaurs. This animal lived along streams, and it is possible that *Coelophysis* ate fish. Its pointed snout would have made fishing easier.

Coelophysis is one of the best known dinosaurs. This is because many *Coelophysis* skeletons were discovered in the Ghost Ranch quarry in northern New Mexico. The tangled remains of hundreds of animals ended up in a single grave.

| 248 | TRIASSIC | 206 | JURASSIC | 144 | CRETACEOUS | 65 MILLION YEARS AGO |

HERRERASAURUS

(huh–RAR–uh–SAHR–uhs)

This early meat-eater probably looked like the later theropod (or meat-eating) dinosaurs. Like them, it walked on its hind legs with its tail held out and off the ground. Like them, it had small forelimbs, a rather short neck, a big head, and a large mouth with sharp teeth.

But there were also differences. *Herrerasaurus* had four toes (a primitive feature). Theropods had three toes. The pelvis and some of the backbones of the *Herrerasaurus* look like those in much later theropods. The pubis (one of the bones of the pelvis) resembles the pubis bone of some later ornithischian dinosaurs. Despite these differences, *Herrerasaurus* is now classified as a theropod.

Herrerasaurus probably lived in a cool, moist world, among groves of ferns and tall conifer trees. Perhaps this dinosaur hunted by springing out from hiding and surprising its prey. When it attacked, it used both its sharp-clawed fingers and cutting teeth.

Herrerasaurus may have been primitive. And yet, it already had qualities needed to survive in a world still ruled by animals other than dinosaurs.

relative size

Herrerasaurus is one of the oldest dinosaurs we know. It lived about 225 million years ago in what is now Argentina, South America.

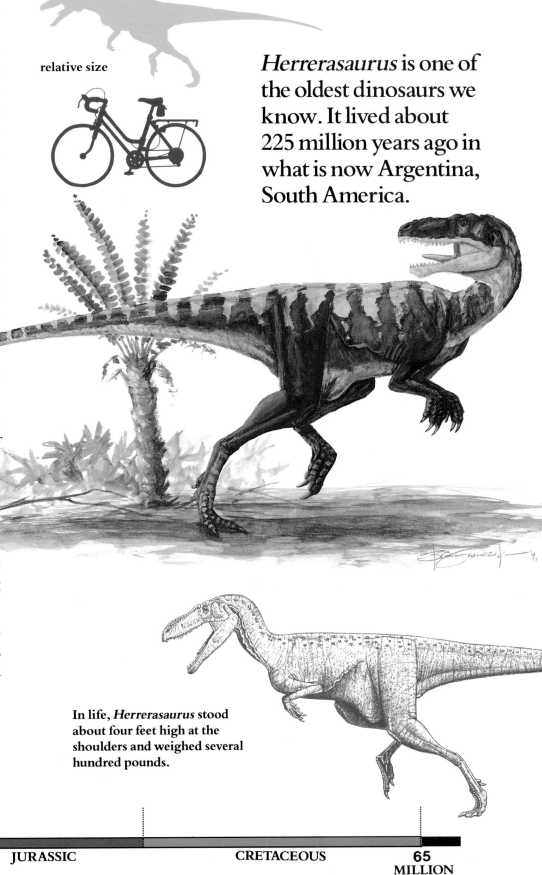

In life, *Herrerasaurus* stood about four feet high at the shoulders and weighed several hundred pounds.

248	TRIASSIC	206	JURASSIC	CRETACEOUS	65 MILLION YEARS AGO

THE JURASSIC WORLD

saw the beginning of the reign of dinosaurs. There were more dinosaurs—and more different kinds of dinosaurs—than in the Triassic Period.

The world was still changing—Pangaea was continuing to break apart. The land was splitting both north and south, and east and west. The land masses began to look like they do now. The continents were drifting apart at a rate of about a quarter inch to three inches a year. These changes in the continents also changed weather patterns. The Jurassic world was dry to semidry, and conifers were the most important land plants. Other plants included ferns, tree ferns, cycads, ginkgos, and horsetails. Ferns served as low ground cover.

Dinosaur evolution was in full swing—they were spreading across the Earth. They appeared in many new and sometimes amazing forms. Mammals were a part of this world, too. But they stayed small and out of the dinosaurs' way.

Two types of pterosaurs shared their world with dinosaurs. Ones with tails died out before the end of the Jurassic, and ones without tails lasted through the Cretaceous.

In the Late Jurassic, small lizards, frogs, and salamanders were crawling along the ground, covered by ferns and other low plants. Turtles had also appeared. Corals, clams, and snails were living in the seas, along with sharks and the marine reptiles, including ichthyosaurs and plesiosaurs.

Dinosaurs adapted to their world and became its rulers. Large plant-eaters, like *Apatosaurus* and *Brachiosaurus,* had long necks to reach the tops of trees for food. Smaller plant-eaters, like *Camptosaurus,* ate the ground cover and small bushes. Small meat-eaters, like *Compsognathus,* probably ate lizards and other small animals. Large meat-eaters, like ferocious *Ceratosaurus,* ate anything they could—maybe even young sauropods.

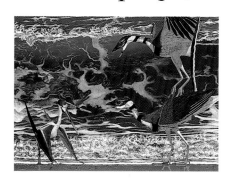

Archaeopteryx, the ancestor of modern birds, flew from conifer tree to conifer tree. Its ancestor may have been a dinosaur; if so, then dinosaurs may have left a living legacy.

The Jurassic Period was an incredibly successful time for dinosaurs, especially for the sauropods. These huge creatures walked the Earth searching for food. Imagine their pounding footsteps echoing in a Jurassic forest!

ALLOSAURUS

(AL-o-SAHR-uhs)

Allosaurus is the best known of all the Late Jurassic theropods. The name of this giant meat-eater means "other reptile."

Allosaurus is mostly known from fossils found in North America. Some remains found in Australia have also been called *Allosaurus*.

With its large skull, powerful neck, massive jaws, daggerlike teeth, powerful limbs, and three-clawed hands, *Allosaurus* and its relatives were the most dangerous meat-eaters of their day. Its large, strong back legs made *Allosaurus* a fast runner. It probably caught prey using its sharp teeth and claws. The curved, pointed finger claws could have held down a victim while *Allosaurus* ate. The dinosaur could not chew, so it probably gulped down meat in chunks.

What did a hunting animal like *Allosaurus* eat? Probably its victims were creatures its size or smaller. An *Allosaurus* menu might include baby or young sauropods, stegosaurs, or ornithopods of any age. Like the lion and other modern-day hunting animals, *Allosaurus* probably also scavenged. This means that if an *Allosaurus* found the body of an animal that died, it probably ate it.

Did *Allosaurus* attack the big sauropods? Probably not, unless the sauropod was sick, very old, or very young. Besides having their size to protect them, sauropods could put up a good fight.

The *Allosaurus* remains found at the Cleveland-Lloyd Quarry show all ages and many sizes. The smallest are little more than three feet long. The average size for adults is about 35 feet. But *Allosaurus* could get much bigger. At least one *Allosaurus* was over 40 feet long—making it as large as the later giant *Tyrannosaurus*.

relative size

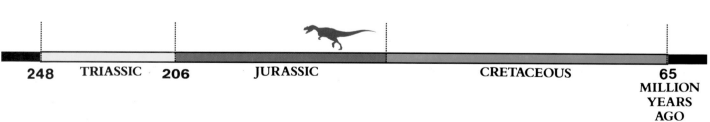

| 248 | TRIASSIC | 206 | JURASSIC | CRETACEOUS | 65 MILLION YEARS AGO |

DIPLODOCUS

(dy-PLO-dah-kus)

All sauropod dinosaurs were long. *Diplodocus* is one of the longest dinosaurs known from complete skeletons. The average length of an adult *Diplodocus* was close to 90 feet. Much of that was its very long neck and tail. This tail ended in a "whiplash" that might have been used as a weapon against theropods.

The name *Diplodocus* means "double beam." This refers to a small piece of bone called a "chevron." Chevrons can be found under each vertebra (the bone of the spine) of the tail. In *Diplodocus*, these chevrons ran forward and backward (like a double beam).

Diplodocus had a small, lightly built head. The nostrils were set on top of the head. All its teeth were at the front of the mouth. These teeth were long, slender, and shaped like pencils. The jaw bones were small and the jaw muscles weak. This tells us that *Diplodocus* probably ate soft plants. With such a long and flexible neck, *Diplodocus* could have eaten ferns that grew on the ground, as well as tall vegetation.

Shiny "gizzard" stones (called gastroliths) have been found in the stomach of some *Diplodocus* skeletons. These stones were swallowed to grind up food.

relative size

Diplodocus has become a fairly common sauropod. Its skeletons are on display at more museums the world over than any other sauropod.

Unlike many other Late Jurassic sauropods, *Diplodocus* was slender. It weighed only about 10 tons. This is about half the weight of its more massive relatives. Maybe being slender helped *Diplodocus* move faster to avoid meat-eaters.

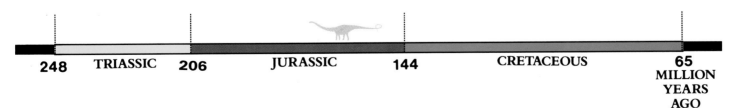

| **248** | **TRIASSIC** | **206** | JURASSIC | **144** | CRETACEOUS | **65** MILLION YEARS AGO |

HETERODONTOSAURUS

(HET-ur-o-DAHNT-o-SAHR-uhs)

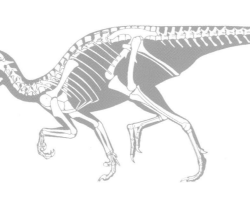

Heterodontosaurus was one of the earliest ornithopod dinosaurs. It lived in South Africa during the Early Jurassic.

relative size

Heterodontosaurus was a fast runner—it needed to get quickly away from large meat-eating dinosaurs.

Heterodontosaurus was a small (only three feet long) dinosaur.

Heterodontosaurus had short, strong front legs. The hands were probably able to grab food. The hind legs were long, with the thigh shorter than either the lower leg or foot. A shorter thigh is a sign that an animal could run fast.

The name *Heterodontosaurus* means "different-toothed reptile." Most dinosaurs had just one kind of tooth. *Heterodontosaurus* had three. The teeth at the front of the mouth were small. They were set on the sides of beaks on both upper and lower jaws. The teeth in the back of the mouth were tall and squared. They were angled so that the upper and lower jaws could meet and grind food. These "cheek teeth" were protected by enamel. This hard material kept the teeth from becoming blunt and dull. It also had two large tusk-like teeth, in both upper and lower jaws. These teeth were set in front of the cheek teeth.

The front teeth were probably used for chopping leaves and stems. The cheek teeth then ground the food. *Heterodontosaurus* probably also had fleshy cheeks to keep the food from falling out of its mouth. The tusks may also have been used in eating. Maybe only a male had these tusks to attract females.

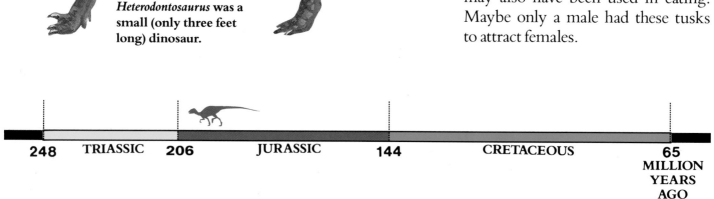

| 248 | TRIASSIC | 206 | JURASSIC | 144 | CRETACEOUS | 65 MILLION YEARS AGO |

LUFENGOSAURUS

(loo–FUNG–o–SAHR–uhs)

Many specimens of *Lufengosaurus* have been found in the People's Republic of China. *Lufengosaurus* was related to *Plateosaurus*, the biggest prosauropod of the Late Triassic.

Lufengosaurus had a small head. Its skull was long and flat. It had a small bony bump on its snout, just above the nostril. The teeth had wide spaces between them. They looked something like blades. The tooth crowns (the part that shows above the gum) were wider at the bottom. Though we believe that it ate plants, the teeth of *Lufengosaurus* were sharp.

Lufengosaurus had strong back legs. Just like its prosauropod relatives, its front legs were shorter than the hind legs. The animal probably walked on all fours. It could rise up on two legs to get at tall plants.

The hands of *Lufengosaurus* had a large thumb with a claw. This was common for prosauropods. Maybe this claw was used as a weapon against other animals, maybe even other *Lufengosaurus* individuals. The claw might also have let this dinosaur spear its food.

Lufengosaurus shared its Early Jurassic world with other animals. The bones of therapsids, early crocodiles, and even mammals have also been found along with it.

Lufengosaurus lived during the Early Jurassic. This dinosaur was named for the Lufeng Basin of Yunnan Province in southwestern China.

relative size

Like *Plateosaurus* (PLAT-ee-o-SAHR-uhs), *Lufengosaurus* was quite large. It was about 20 feet long. This animal had a very long neck.

There were other prosauropods, too, including one bigger than *Lufengosaurus*. It was named *Yunnanosaurus* (yoo-NAN-o-SAHR-uhs), after the Yunnan Province in China.

| 248 | TRIASSIC | 206 | JURASSIC | 144 | CRETACEOUS | 65 MILLION YEARS AGO |

MAMENCHISAURUS

(mah-MEN-chee-SAHR-uhs)

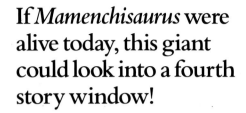

If *Mamenchisaurus* were alive today, this giant could look into a fourth story window!

relative size

Mamenchisaurus is the largest sauropod known from China. Its weight may have been 10 to 20 tons. *Mamenchisaurus* seems to have been rather slender compared to other sauropds. Maybe it was graceful when it walked.

One of the most spectacular-looking sauropods was *Mamenchisaurus*. Try to imagine an animal whose neck was almost as long as its entire body! *Mamenchisaurus* was a Late Jurassic sauropod that was about 72 feet long. Its neck was about 33 feet long.

This long neck can be explained by two things. The vertebrae (or bones in the spine) were longer than usual, and *Mamenchisaurus* had more vertebrae. If we add the length of the shoulders, we can picture the neck of *Mamenchisaurus* raising its head some 44 feet off the ground.

Mamenchisaurus remains have been found in the People's Republic of China. It was named after Mamenchi, the place of its discovery. ("Chi" means "brook," and "Mamen" was the name of the brook.)

Fossil bones believed to be dragons were collected at this site. These so-called "dragon bones" were ground into powder and sold as medicine. It was believed that "dragon bones" could cure sicknesses. Fortunately, *Mamenchisaurus* did not end up on medicine shelves.

Similarities can be seen between *Mamenchisaurus* and *Diplodocus*. Because of those resemblances, scientists can see a relationship between sauropods of China and of North America and Europe. This tells us that a piece of land may have connected these areas during the Late Jurassic.

248	TRIASSIC	206	JURASSIC	144	CRETACEOUS	65 MILLION YEARS AGO

SCELIDOSAURUS

(skee-LY-do-SAHR-uhs)

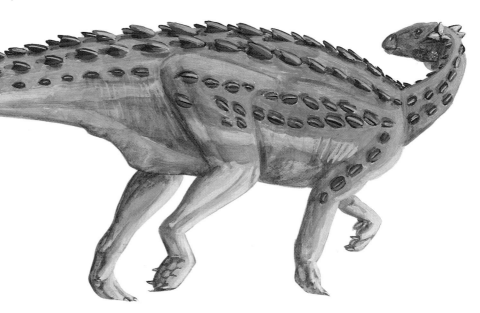

Scelidosaurus was one of the oldest ornithischians of the Early Jurassic. It was first found in southern England and described in 1860. It was a very complete skeleton with the bones still connected (or articulated).

Scelidosaurus was one of the earliest members of the group called the Thyreophora. Its later relatives included the plated stegosaurs and armored ankylosaurs.

Scelidosaurus was a heavily built animal. Its head was large. The teeth were simple and leaf-shaped. *Scelidosaurus* probably ate the leaves of shrubs and branches that grew near the ground.

The most unusual thing about *Scelidosaurus* was its armor. In life, the skin had many small bony plates in it. These plates could be found on the animal's back, sides, and tail. They probably protected the animal from meat-eaters.

Recently, new specimens of *Scelidosaurus* have been found. These specimens also show fossil skin impressions. From these impressions we know that the skin of this dinosaur had small, rounded scales. These are important in understanding how a dinosaur may have looked.

The name *Scelidosaurus* means "limb reptile." The dinosaur was named that because of its large legs. It walked on all four legs, and each foot had four toes.

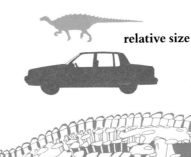

relative size

The tail of *Scelidosaurus* was longer than most other ornithischian dinosaur tails.

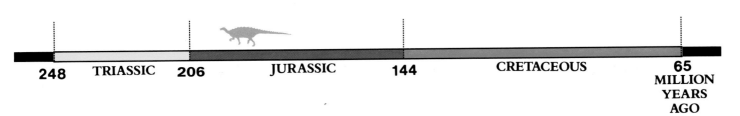

| 248 | TRIASSIC | 206 | JURASSIC | 144 | CRETACEOUS | 65 MILLION YEARS AGO |

SHUNOSAURUS

(SHOO-no-SAHR-uhs)

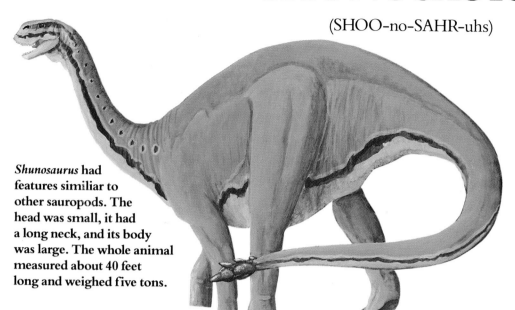

Shunosaurus had features similiar to other sauropods. The head was small, it had a long neck, and its body was large. The whole animal measured about 40 feet long and weighed five tons.

relative size

In paleontology, some of the most exciting discoveries are completely surprising. One such discovery was made with *Shunosaurus*, a Middle Jurassic sauropod.

Future dinosaur discoveries will tell us whether *Omeisaurus* (O-mee-SAHR-uhs) also had a tail club like *Shunosaurus*.

The name *Shunosaurus* comes from "Shuo," the Chinese word for "Sichuan." So far, more than 20 almost-complete skeletons of this dinosaur have been collected in the Lower Shaximiao Formation of Sichuan Province in the People's Republic of China. Five good skulls were also found, which is rare.

The skull of *Shunosaurus* was rather short (something like that of the North American *Camarasaurus*). *Shunosaurus* had many slender teeth.

But skeletons of *Shunosaurus* revealed something new and unexpected. Of the many *Shunosaurus* skeletons collected, some had a most unusual feature. The tail ended in a large club of bone. Jutting out from this club, there may have been two pairs of short spikes.

What was this tail club used for? Perhaps, like the tail clubs of the armored ankylosaurs, it was used as a weapon. The long tail of *Shunosaurus* could be swung with great force. The club could have hurt meat-eating dinosaurs that lived in the same time and place.

Was *Shunosaurus* the only sauropod to have a bony club on its tail? Might other sauropods also have had such clubs? Another Chinese sauropod, the very long-necked *Omeisaurus*, may have carried a tail club.

| 248 | TRIASSIC | 206 | JURASSIC | 144 | CRETACEOUS | 65 MILLION YEARS AGO |

STEGOSAURUS

(STEG-o-SAHR-uhs)

Stegosaurus is the largest of the stegosaurs. It is also one of the most famous of all dinosaurs. This dinosaur is well known for the triangular plates on its back and the spikes on its tail. Some of these plates were quite large. *Stegosaurus* means "roofed reptile."

This animal walked on all four legs. Because its head was held low, *Stegosaurus* probably ate what grew close to the ground. The highest point of the dinosaur's body was at its hips. There the animal was about 10 feet tall. The largest of its back plates was located above the hips. This plate added height to the dinosaur.

Its small head had weak jaws. There were no teeth in the front of the jaws, but there was a beak for chopping vegetation. The teeth on the sides of the jaws were leaf-shaped. These teeth had grooves for crushing food.

A tail specimen with the spikes in place show that these were paired. The spikes must have made a deadly weapon when the tail was swung at meat-eaters like *Allosaurus*.

The brain of *Stegosaurus* may have been small, but so was its head. Compared to body size, the brain of this dinosaur is bigger than that of the sauropods.

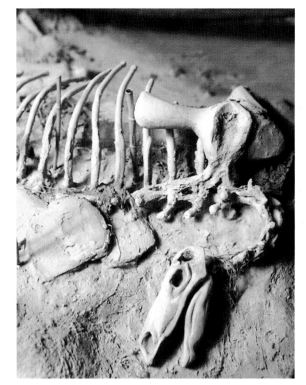

The plates on the back were set in two rows. There has been much debate about the arrangement of the plates. Were they set in pairs, one alongside the other? Most paleontologists think they alternated. No two plates were the same size, so they cannot be arranged in pairs. One *Stegosaurus* skeleton was found with the plates still in place. These plates were in an alternating position.

Stegosaurus was discovered in 1877 in Colorado. It was one of the first dinosaurs known from almost complete skeletons.

relative size

Stegosaurus was about 20 to 24 feet long. It weighed at least two tons.

| 248 | TRIASSIC | 206 | JURASSIC | 144 | CRETACEOUS | 65 MILLION YEARS AGO |

THE CRETACEOUS WORLD

 was filled with fantastic dinosaurs that had amazing features. The reign of sauropods on the northern continents was almost over by the beginning of Cretaceous. Other dinosaurs were taking their place as the world's most common plant-eaters.

One thing that probably caused this change was that the first flowering plants began to appear. These plants offered a new source of food. At first, these plants grew low to the ground and grew quickly. Later, some of them became familiar hardwood trees, such as poplar, oak, and maple.

The ornithopods, a group including many different plant-eaters, thrived on these new plants. This group included the hadrosaurs, or duckbilled dinosaurs.

The Cretaceous was, in fact, more "modern." The continents were moving nearer to their positions of today, though at the beginning of the period, the land masses were still close together. The Rocky Mountains began to rise. Volcanoes were erupting often.

Seas divided flooded continents; one sea divided the North American continent in two. Toward the end of the the Cretaceous, this sea (called the Interior Seaway) drained off. The climate was generally warm and humid, with much rainfall. At the end were cooler temperatures and more definite seasons.

Huge reptiles ruled the seas, and large pterosaurs owned the skies. But birds and other more modern types of animals, such as small furry mammals, were common.

There seem to have been more dinosaurs than ever in the Late Cretaceous. They were also some of the most unusual, with frills and crests and horns. This is when the largest and most ferocious meat-eaters lived.

Among the new breeds of dinosaurs were the ceratopsians (or horned dinosaurs). Ceratopsians began as small, almost hornless forms. Larger forms had huge skulls with spectacular bony frills.

The pachycephalosaurs (or "bonehead" dinosaurs) seem to be related to the ceratopsians. The armored ankylosaurs appeared, some of which carried heavy bone clubs on their tails. New theropods were fighting for existence, some with bull-like horns (*Carnotaurus*), or back "fins" (*Spinosaurus*), or gigantic arms (*Deinocheirus*). The Cretaceous was the period of greatest success for dinosaurs.

ABELISAURUS

(AH-bel-i-SAHR-uhs)

Although *Abelisaurus* was probably from 25 to 30 feet long, we can only guess at the animal's true length. All that has been found so far is the dinosaur's skull.

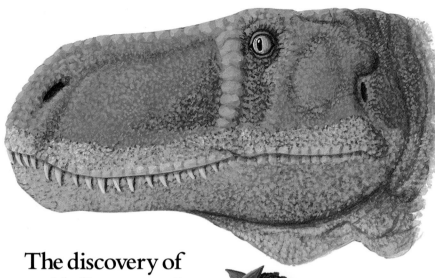

The discovery of *Abelisaurus* and *Carnotaurus* have given paleontologists a better understanding of South American theropods.

relative size

Carnotaurus (whose name means "meat-eating bull") had two bull-like horns on its head and very tiny frontlimbs. Like *Abelisaurus*, *Carnotaurus* was found in South America. *Abelisaurus* may actually be a descendant of *Carnotaurus*.

Abelisaurus (named after a scientist named Abel) was a large theropod dinosaur that lived in what is now Patagonia, Argentina, South America, during the Late Cretaceous.

The skull of *Abelisaurus* is about three feet long. The skull at first looks like the much bigger skull of *Tyrannosaurus*. But on closer look, we can see that the *Abelisaurus* skull is quite different. One difference is the much larger openings in front of the eye openings (or orbits).

Abelisaurus is so different from other theropods that it has been placed in its own family. Another member of its family is the strange *Carnotaurus* (CAR-no-TAHR-uhs), a theropod dinosaur known from a very complete skeleton.

In the Cretaceous, dinosaurs that lived in southern parts of the world were very different from their relatives in the north. During the earlier Jurassic period, the northern and southern land masses separated. This separation resulted in some changes. Dinosaurs like *Abelisaurus* and *Carnotaurus* were cut off from the northern theropods. A relative of *Abelisaurus* named *Majungatholus* was recently found in Madagascar. Left on their own, these animals evolved in their own ways, adapting to the conditions of their southern world.

| 248 | TRIASSIC | 206 | JURASSIC | 144 | CRETACEOUS | 65 MILLION YEARS AGO |

DEINONYCHUS

(dy-NON-ick-us)

Remains of *Deinonychus* were discovered in southern Montana in 1964. Dr. John H. Ostrom, the Yale University paleontologist who studied and named this theropod, saw that it was different. *Deinonychus* proved to be so different that it changed how we thought about dinosaurs.

The head of *Deinonychus* was quite large compared to its body, as were the heads of most meat-eating dinosaurs. Its brain was very large compared to its body. The small sharp teeth were pointed back and were designed for holding and biting prey. The arms were fairly long. The hands had three fingers, each finger ending in a large claw. The fingers were able to move so that the animal could use them during an attack. The tail was stiffened by long, thin bony rods. These rods helped the tail balance the body.

The most amazing thing about *Deinonychus* was the hind foot. The claw on the inner toes was very large. It was also sharply pointed and very curved.

With an understanding of *Deinonychus*, scientists began to look at dinosaurs in a new way. The image of dinosaurs being stupid and slow was reconsidered. Today we view many dinosaurs as quick and intelligent.

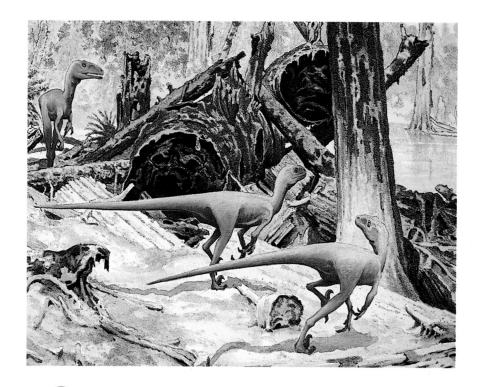

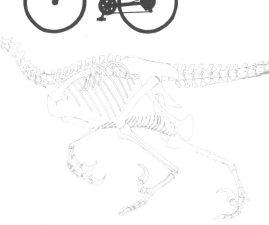

relative size

The sickle claw of *Deinonychus* was a deadly weapon, ready to go into action.

Deinonychus may have been rather small. This dinosaur was just 8 to 10 feet long and 3 feet high at the hips. Still, this theropod was a terror in the Early Cretaceous.

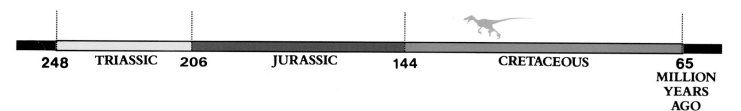

| 248 | TRIASSIC | 206 | JURASSIC | 144 | CRETACEOUS | 65 MILLION YEARS AGO |

EUOPLOCEPHALUS

(YOO-o-plo-SEF-uh-lus)

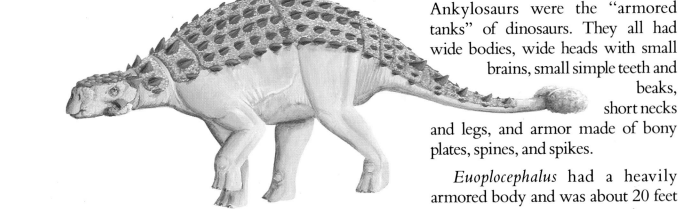

Ankylosaurs were the "armored tanks" of dinosaurs. They all had wide bodies, wide heads with small brains, small simple teeth and beaks, short necks and legs, and armor made of bony plates, spines, and spikes.

Euoplocephalus had a heavily armored body and was about 20 feet long. It ate plants growing close to the ground.

No specimen of *Euoplocephalus* has yet been found with its armor in place. However, we do know that it had a lot of armor on the head and body. Even the eyelids were protected by bone. Its name means "well-armored head."

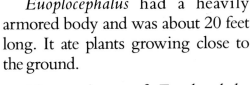

Top: The Asian *Saichania* **(sy-CHAYN-ee-uh) was closely related to** *Euoplocephalus.* **Above:** *Euoplocephalus***'s bony club-like tail made an effective weapon.**

Euoplocephalus also had a weapon. The tail of this dinosaur was long and probably was carried straight out and off the ground. At the end of the tail was the heavy, bony club. This club made a dangerous weapon.

Paleontologists think that *Euoplocephalus* may have had a good sense of smell. The air passages inside this dinosaur's nostrils were looped. This tells us that many nerves for smell were probably there. Another idea about these looped passages is that they were used to make a noise like a bugle to communicate with others of its kind.

Ankylosaurs were among the last of the dinosaurs—some kinds lived until the very end of the Cretaceous Period.

relative size

248	TRIASSIC	206	JURASSIC	144	CRETACEOUS	65 MILLION YEARS AGO

IGUANODON

(i-GWAHN-o-DAHN)

Groups of almost complete *Iguanodon* skeletons were found in both Belgium and Germany. These skeletons were different ages and sizes.

Iguanodon walked on heavy back legs. The body was balanced by a tail stiffened by bony tendons. If it wanted to, the animal could come down on all fours and use its strong arms for walking. The head had a blunt snout covered by horn, perfect for cropping leaves, small branches, and shoots. This food would then be torn apart by the many cheek teeth in the back of the jaws.

The hands of *Iguanodon* are interesting. They had blunt hooves (something like a horse's or cow's) that could be used in walking or resting. There was a small outer finger that could have been using in grasping vegetation. An unusual spikelike bone belonging to *Iguanodon* was, at first, thought to be a nose horn. It turned out to be a large, spikelike thumb. This thumb could have been used as a weapon against meat-eating dinosaurs. It might also have been used during contests between rival *Iguanodon* males— fighting over territory, food and water, or females.

Iguanodon was the second dinosaur (after *Megalosaurus*) to be named and scientifically described.

Iguanodon was a large ornithopod. Adults were as long as 33 feet, and they weighed about six tons! *Iguanodon* looked much different than what scientists first thought it looked like. They thought it looked like a cross between an iguana and a rhinoceros.

relative size

248	TRIASSIC	206	JURASSIC	144	CRETACEOUS	65

MILLION
YEARS
AGO

MAIASAURA

(MY-ah-SAHR-ah)

A hatchling *Maiasaura* had a tall, narrow head and big eyes. Even by today's standards, the babies were cute. As the baby grew, the head got lower and wider from front to back. A wide horny beak developed.

Maiasaura is an important and famous discovery. It was found in the Two Medicine Formation of western Montana in 1978. Scientists had believed that dinosaurs laid their eggs and left them. *Maiasaura* cared for its young.

Maiasaura was a flat-headed hadrosaur (or duckbilled dinosaur). It was a large animal, measuring about 30 feet long. Its face was long and somewhat narrow, and there was a low bony crest over the eyes.

The mother *Maiasaura* laid her eggs in a large nest of dirt or mud that measured about six feet across. The eggs, between 15 and 24, were laid in a circular or spiral pattern. The eggs were about 6 inches long. The mother covered the eggs with plants. The rotting (or composting) plants gave off heat that incubated the eggs (made them hatch).

Maiasaura hatchlings were about 15 inches long. Unlike some other known dinosaur hatchlings, these babies were not able to take care of themselves. A young *Maiasaura* probably stayed in the nest for a few months. During this time, it grew to about four feet long. When it reached about eight feet, it was big enough to join the herd.

John Horner and Robert Makela gave this dinosaur its name for a very good reason. *Maiasaura* means "good mother reptile."

relative size

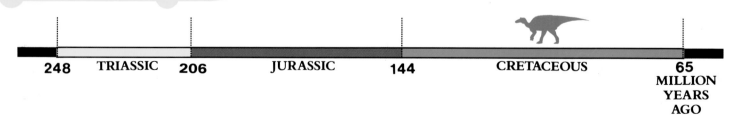

| 248 | TRIASSIC | 206 | JURASSIC | 144 | CRETACEOUS | 65 MILLION YEARS AGO |

PACHYRHINOSAURUS

(PAK-ee-RYN-o-SAHR-uhs)

Like other ceratopsians, *Pachyrhinosaurus* had a massive head. (Only the heads of *Pentaceratops*, *Torosaurus*, and *Triceratops* were bigger.) Its face was long and rather flattened. It had a short beak and a short frill. The frill had two large openings (called "fenestrae"). Bony spikes of different sizes ran along the border of the frill. These included two very large spikes toward the top. Most unusual were the structures that stood straight out from the middle of the frill.

Instead of having horns on the face (like *Triceratops* and other large ceratopsians), *Pachyrhinosaurus* had a very thick "boss" (a thick, bumpy pad of bone). This boss ran from the front of its snout back to above the eyes. *Pachyrhinosaurus* means "thick-nose reptile."

Did *Pachyrhinosaurus* once have a horn that had broken off? Was this boss really what was left of that horn? Was it a scar? The answers came in 1985 when a large bonebed (a place containing a large number of bones of the same kind of animal) with many adult and juvenile *Pachyrhinosaurus* specimens was discovered in Alberta. These specimens proved that the boss was a normal feature.

In 1988, the remains of *Pachyrhinosaurus* were found on the north slope of Alaska.

Pachyrhinosaurus may have used its boss to push over trees so it could get to the top leaves.

relative size

The most unusual of all known ceratopsians was probably *Pachyrhinosaurus*. This 21-foot-long animal was quite different from its horned cousins.

| 248 | TRIASSIC | 206 | JURASSIC | 144 | CRETACEOUS | 65 MILLION YEARS AGO |

SEGNOSAURUS

(SEG-no-SAHR-uhs)

The discovery of *Seg-nosaurus*, in the Gobi Desert of Mongolia, was one of the most important dinosaur finds of the 1970s. It was found during an expedition by Russian and Mongolian scientists. For a time, scientists thought *Segnosaurus* represented a whole new group of Late Cretaceous dinosaurs.

Segnosaurus, whose name means "slow reptile," was indeed a curious kind of dinosaur. Although it was a theropod, its bones showed a strange mix of features.

It is now clear that *Segnosaurus* was a theropod, and its small, sharp teeth and long, slender claws were like those of theropods. In some ways, however, these teeth were more like those in prosauropods than theropods. Unlike other theropods but like ornithopods, *Segnosaurus* had no teeth in the front of its jaws.

The limbs of *Segnosaurus* were heavy and the feet wide. At first, paleontologists weren't sure where *Segnosaurus* and its relatives fit in dinosaur classification. Some had thought of *Segnosaurians* as being late descendants of the earlier prosauropods. More recently we know that *Segnosaurus* and other segnosaurians were theropods, albeit strange ones.

relative size

Unlike other theropods, the feet of *Segnosaurus* had four toes instead of three.

Another segnosaurian, called *Erlikosaurus* (AYR-lik-o-SAHR-uhs), seems to have had a prosauropodlike beak. *Segnosaurus* might also have had a beak.

248	TRIASSIC	206	JURASSIC	144	CRETACEOUS	65

MILLION
YEARS
AGO

38

TENONTOSAURUS

(te-NAHN-to-SAHR-uhs)

A large number of *Tenontosaurus* bones have been collected since the first skeleton was found in Big Horn County, Montana, in 1903. So far, dozens of skeletons of this dinosaur have been found in Montana and Wyoming. Some of these were only partial skeletons, others were almost complete. Eight juvenile skeletons have been found, but most were either half grown or almost fully grown adults.

Tenontosaurus was a common large ornithopod living in North America during the Early Cretaceous. It is also one of the best known of all dinosaurs.

Much of the length of *Tenontosaurus* was taken up by its very long tail. In fact, two-thirds of the animal's length was its tail. This tail was stiffened by "ossified tendons." (Tendons are bands of tough tissue that connect muscles to bones. Ossified means that these tendons had become bone.) *Tenontosaurus* usually walked on its hind legs, and these ossified tendons helped keep its tail out straight. The long tail was kept off the ground when the animal walked and helped to balance the front of the body. *Tenontosaurus* means "tendon reptile."

Tenontosaurus had a rather small head and a long, flexible neck. As in most other ornithopod dinosaurs, there were no teeth in the front of the mouth. Instead, there was a horny beak for biting off plants. Its strong, tightly fitted teeth were made for grinding up tough plants.

Smaller and more slender than its relative *Iguanodon*, *Tenontosaurus* was a medium-size ornithopod. The dinosaur probably weighed about 1,000 pounds. The average length of this animal was about 22 feet.

relative size

| 248 | TRIASSIC | 206 | JURASSIC | 144 | CRETACEOUS | 65 MILLION YEARS AGO |

TROODON

(TRO-o-don)

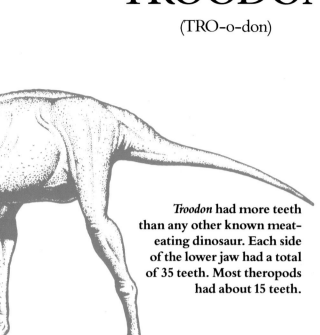

Troodon had more teeth than any other known meat-eating dinosaur. Each side of the lower jaw had a total of 35 teeth. Most theropods had about 15 teeth.

Troodon was a small theropod of the Late Cretaceous. Its skeleton was about six feet long.

This was the first dinosaur to be named in North America. It was named in 1856 by Joseph Leidy. *Troodon* means "wounding tooth." The first specimen of *Troodon* found was just one tooth. The specimen was collected in the Judith River area of what was then called the Nebraska Territory (now Montana). Leidy at first thought the tooth was from a prehistoric lizard. Since that original discovery, more and better *Troodon* specimens have been found.

This dinosaur had huge eyes that took up a big part of its skull. With these eyes, the animal could probably have seen in dim twilight. Eyes like these would have let *Troodon* hunt prey that other theropods, with poorer vision, might never even see.

The hands of *Troodon* had slender fingers. The inner finger had a big, thin, pointed, sharp claw.

The second toe of the foot was similar to the toe of *Deinonychus*. It had a large sickle claw for slashing prey. Unlike the "terrible claw" in *Deinonychus*, the claw of *Troodon* was smaller and higher up on the foot. It was also smaller than the very large claw of its hand.

Troodon had a very large brain. The brain would have been about six times bigger than that of a crocodile the same size.

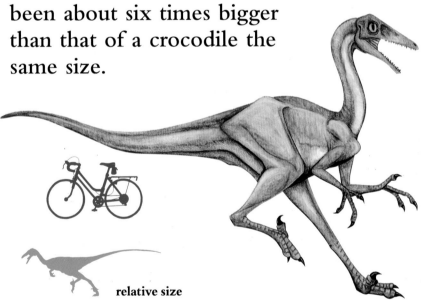

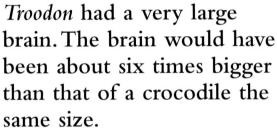

relative size

| 248 | TRIASSIC | 206 | JURASSIC | 144 | CRETACEOUS | 65 |

MILLION YEARS AGO

TYRANNOSAURUS

(ty-RAN-o-SAHR-uhs)

One of the last dinosaurs, and almost everyone's favorite, is *Tyrannosaurus*. *Tyrannosaurus rex* means "tyrant reptile king."

Tyrannosaurus stalked its prey on powerful hind legs. Some paleontologists believe that these legs were made for fast running, and that the animal could have run over 30 miles an hour! Whether running or just walking, *Tyrannosaurus* was one of the biggest and most powerful meat-eating animals that ever lived.

For many years, specimens of this dinosaur were very rare. In recent years, more *Tyrannosaurus* remains have been found. Two almost complete skeletons were collected in 1990—one in Montana, the other in South Dakota. During the summer of 2001, five more Montana *Tyrannosaurus* skeletons were collected.

Tyrannosaurus is famous for its very short arms. These front limbs were much shorter than those of earlier theropods, such as *Allosaurus*. While *Allosaurus* and its relatives had three fingers on each hand, *Tyrannosaurus* only had two.

Some paleontologists thought that these limbs were completely useless. One of the recently found *Tyrannosaurus* skeletons includes a complete front leg and hand. Now we know that the upper arm bone of this dinosaur was quite massive, and that the lower arm bones were very short. Although tiny, the forelimbs of this dinosaur were indeed strong.

Just imagine a meat-eating creature measuring 40 feet long and weighing six tons. Its head, big as a refrigerator, was held as high as a split-level house. The mouth, more than a yard long, was filled with sharp teeth, some as long as 6 inches.

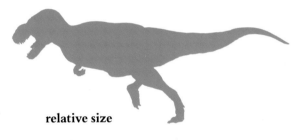

relative size

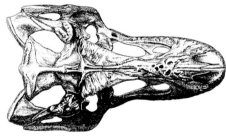

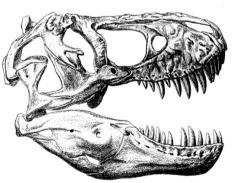

The brain of *Tyrannosaurus* was quite large. *Tyrannosaurus* had the biggest brain of any dinosaur. Its brain was even larger than the brain of a gorilla or chimpanzee.

| 248 | TRIASSIC | 206 | JURASSIC | 144 | CRETACEOUS | 65 MILLION YEARS AGO |

DINOSAUR EXTINCTION

has baffled scientists for years. But one thing they know—dinosaurs were the most amazingly successful animals ever. They were dominant for about 160 million years. Did dinosaurs become extinct because of a single event, or did it happen over time?

Did dinosaurs die because the world got too hot or too cold? Did a giant comet hit earth? There are many theories—but no certain answers yet. Dinosaurs were not the only animals to become extinct. Why didn't all plants and animals die? We may never find out.

The most important fact about dinosaurs is their success, not their extinction. Imagine, humans have lived for less than 2 million years. Not only did these fantastic creatures live for millions of years, but they continue to live in our imagination!